W9-CIB-628

AMERICANA MAZES

Dave Phillips

Dover Publications, Inc. Mineola, New York

Introduction:

Americana Mazes celebrates American icons—symbols that represent the ideals, history, and shared experiences of a culture. A maze is a metaphor for a journey—from the past to a present day appreciation of a shared bond. So I carefully drew paths for the mazes in this book to form pictures that represent milestones in American history and symbols that are uniquely American. See how many pictures you can recognize along the way, and what they represent. I have included a short caption for each maze but I encourage you to learn much more of the story that each maze represents. And, of course, have fun finding your way through each maze! If you need any help along the way, a solutions section begins on page 37.

Copyright

Copyright © 2011 by Dave Phillips
All rights reserved.

Bibliographical Note

Americana Mazes is a new work, first published by
Dover Publications, Inc., in 2011.

International Standard Book Number

ISBN-13: 978-0-486-48108-1
ISBN-10: 0-486-48108-5

Manufactured in the United States by LSC Communications
48108504   2016
www.doverpublications.com

1. Map of the USA
The United States of America stretches across the North American continent from the Atlantic Ocean to the Pacific Ocean (from sea to shining sea). Including the states of Alaska and Hawaii (not included on the map) there are currently 50 states in the Union.

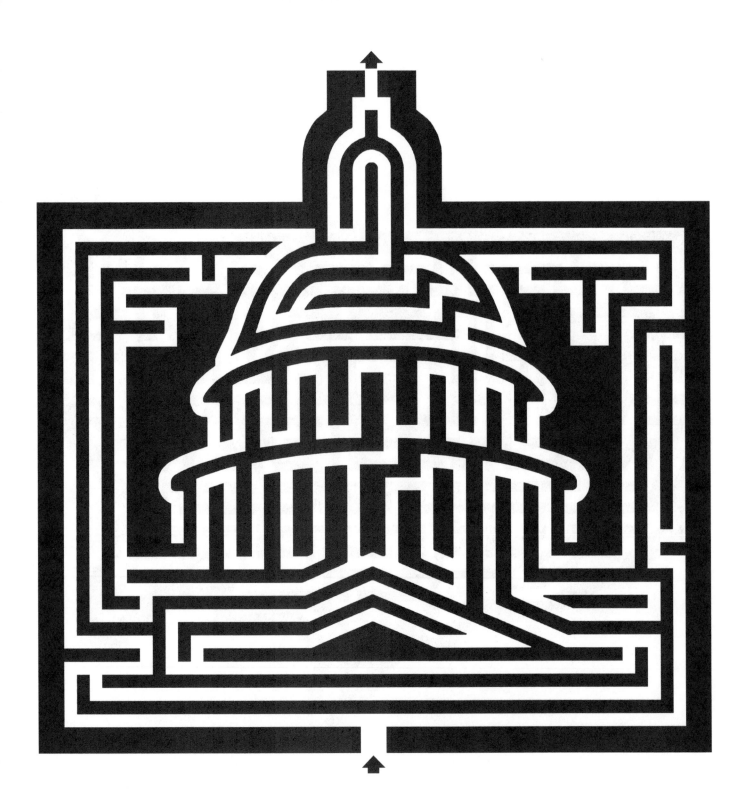

2. The US Capitol

The United States Capitol building in Washington DC is the home of the Senate and House of Representatives. These two "houses" form the legislative branch of government, which along with the President (executive branch) and the Courts (judicial branch), makes the laws by which we live.

3. American Bald Eagle
The majestic bald eagle is the symbol for the United States and is found on seals, monuments, and coins. Though this beautiful bird remains endangered, it is making a comeback. It is illegal to own or even pick up an eagle feather since this encourages the killing of bald eagles for profit.

4. Route 66
Route 66 is called America's highway. Though only parts of it remain intact, it remains an American icon representing the freedom of the road and the nostalgia of the early days of the automobile. It stretched from Chicago to Los Angeles through Illinois, Missouri, Kansas, Oklahoma, Texas, New Mexico, Arizona, and California.

5. Sheriff's Badge

The election of a person to serve as a sheriff (the leader of a police force) is an almost uniquely American tradition. Of the 50 states, only three do not have sheriffs; they are: Alaska, Hawaii, and Connecticut. The star associated with the sheriff's badge is traditionally a magic talisman (token) against evil forces.

6. Country Square Dancing

Although common throughout Europe as far back as the 17th century, square dancing has become a uniquely American dance due to the evolution of immigrant folk dances. Nineteen US states have designated it as their official state dance.

7. Rodeo
Rodeo is a sport that came from the working practices of cattle herding. It is based on the skills required by cowboys (and cowgirls), which include roping, steer wrestling, and bareback bronco and bull riding. Rodeo is most popular in the western United States.

8. Buffalo

The American bison is commonly known as the buffalo. The buffalo once roamed the American grassland in vast herds that shook the earth as they moved. American Indians hunted them for food and for their sturdy hides. Once an endangered species, buffalo herds are now rebounding.

9. Silver Dollar

The American silver dollar was first released in 1794 and was America's favorite coin throughout the nineteenth century. Though dollar coins are not used today, the silver dollar remains a collector's favorite and an American icon.

10. Jack-o'-Lantern
A scary or funny face carved into a pumpkin is a uniquely American tradition associated with harvest season and later became an emblem for Halloween, an unofficial American holiday. A candle inside the carved pumpkin lights it from inside creating an eerie effect.

11. Lighthouse

Dotting both coasts, American lighthouses are icons recalling earlier days of seafaring. They are beloved monuments and subjects of artistic expression. The first American lighthouse came to life in 1716 in Boston Harbor.

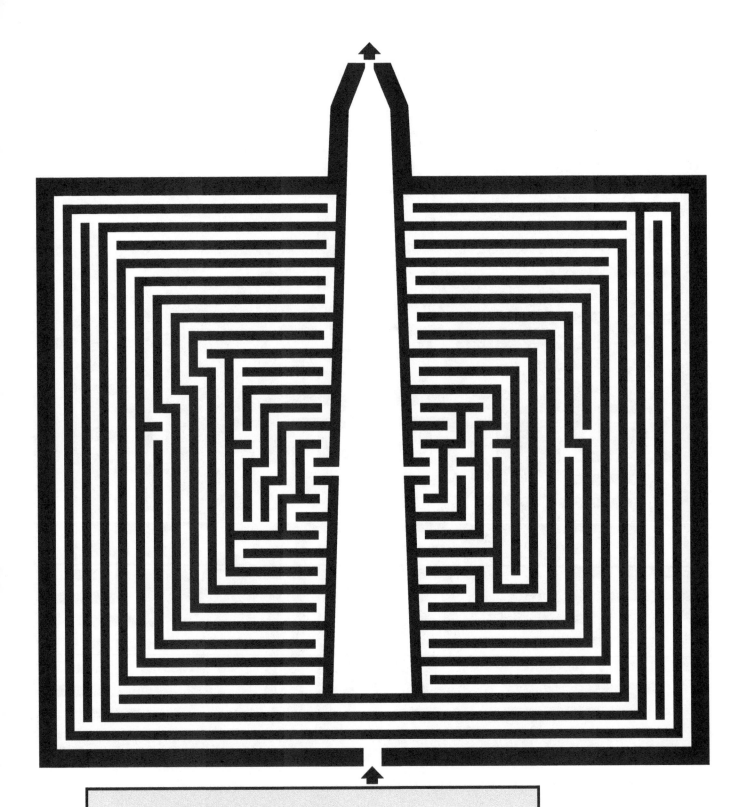

12. The Washington Monument
The Washington Monument was built as a monument to the first U.S. president, General George Washington. It is the tallest structure in Washington D.C. and the world's tallest obelisk.

13. George Washington
Called the "Father of our Country," George Washington lived between 1732 and 1799. He is revered foremost as the commander of the Continental Army that won American independence from Great Britain.

14. Minuteman
A Minuteman was a select member of the militia during the American Revolutionary War. Minutemen were highly mobile and ready to respond immediately to British threats, which is how they earned their name.

15. Lewis & Clark

The Lewis and Clark Expedition (1804–1806) was the first overland exploration commissioned by the newly formed United States. The goal of the westward expedition was to catalog the resources gained by the Louisiana Purchase.

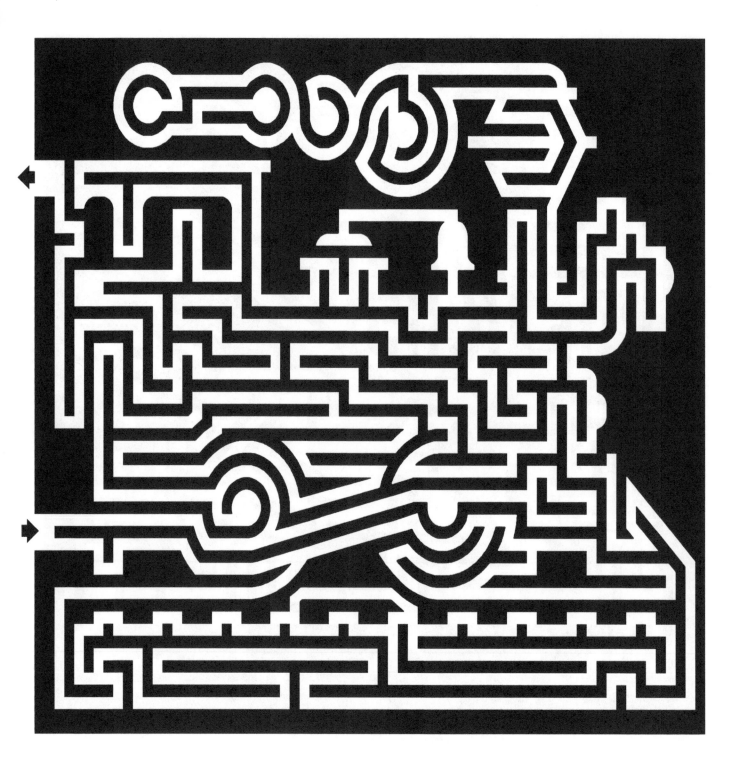

16. American Railroad

There was a time when railroads connected every small town and large city in America. Halfway through the 20th century, however, railroads went into decline as a way to transport people and goods. Today, rail lines, landmarks, and train stations are being preserved as part of our national heritage and for recreation.

17. Jamestown

Jamestown was founded in the Virginia Colony on May 14, 1607. It is regarded as the first permanent British settlement in the United States. The *Susan Constant*, *Godspeed* and *Discovery* were the ships that brought the settlers safely across the Atlantic Ocean.

18. Baseball
Called "America's Pastime," baseball evolved in the middle of the 19th century. The first recorded baseball game was played in 1846 at the Elysian Fields, in Hoboken, New Jersey.

19. Football

American Football is a tough contact game that dominates American sports. It is played by high school, college, and professional teams. The first recorded college game took place in 1869 when Rutgers defeated Princeton.

20. Martin Luther King Jr.
Martin Luther King Jr. is an icon from the civil rights movement of the early 1960's. King led the 1963 March on Washington where he delivered his famous "I Have a Dream" speech.

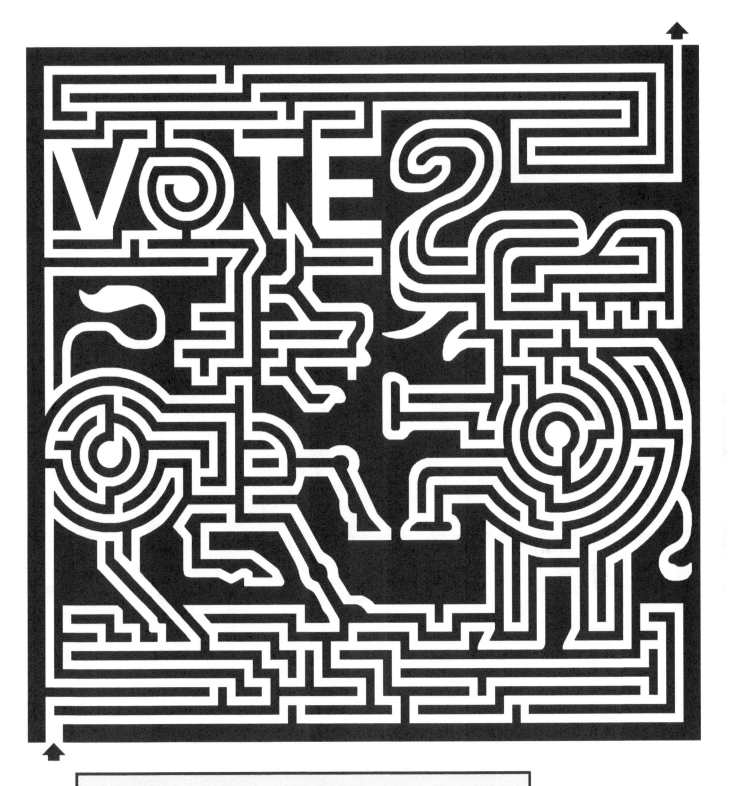

21. Right to Vote
Americans earned the right of self-governance by opposing British taxation without representation. There are two political parties: The Democrats who have a donkey as a mascot and the Republicans whose mascot is an elephant.

22. Sitting Bull
Sitting Bull is famous for his role in the American Indian victory at the Battle of the Little Bighorn against Lt. Colonel Custer and the US 7th Cavalry on June 25, 1876. He also toured as a performer in Buffalo Bill's Wild West Show.

23. The Stagecoach

Before the coming of the railroad, and long before the automobile, the stagecoach was the premier mode of travel throughout the United States. Valuables such as gold, as well as passengers, rode bumpy dirt roads while a man rode "shotgun" to protect against bandits.

24. First Flight

The Wright brothers, Orville and Wilbur, are Americans generally credited with inventing and building the first successful airplane. On December 17, 1903 they flew a powered manned craft at Kill Devil Hills, North Carolina.

25. Amelia Earhart
Amelia Earhart was the first woman to fly solo across the Atlantic Ocean. She was an American aviation pioneer and author who wrote best-selling books about her flying experiences. She went missing July 2, 1937.

26. Abraham Lincoln
Abraham Lincoln was the 16th President of the United States. He successfully led the country through its greatest internal crisis, the Civil War, preserving the Union and ending slavery.

27. The Civil War
The American Civil War (1861–1865) was also known as the War Between the States. Eleven Southern states broke away from the Union to form the Confederate States of America. The war ended slavery in America and preserved a nation indivisible.

28. American Soldier

The modern American soldier fights for our freedom. The men and women of the armed forces join voluntarily to proudly serve the Nation. The five branches of the military are: The Army, Air Force, Navy, Marine Corps, and Coast Guard.

29. Paul Revere

The famous "Midnight Ride" of Paul Revere occurred on the night of April 18/19, 1775. He rode from Boston to Lexington to warn John Hancock and Samuel Adams of the advancing British army.

30. Elvis Presley

Elvis Presley was one of the most popular American singers and performers of the 20th century. He died in 1977, but is still remembered as a cultural icon and often called "the King."

31. The Liberty Bell

The Liberty Bell is one of the best known symbols of freedom and independence. It was proudly rung to announce the opening of the First Continental Congress in 1774 and after the Battle of Lexington during the American Revolution in 1775.

32. American Indians
American Indians are peoples who inhabited America before Europeans discovered and colonized what they referred to as "The New World." Today, many American Indians have a unique relationship with the United States since they live in nations or tribes independent from the government.

33. The Wild West
The American Wild West, often referred to as the Old West, is generally anywhere in the continental United States west of the Mississippi River during the latter half of the 19th century. It was called wild due to the rough living conditions and the harsh way of life often won at the point of a gun.

34. American Farming
The United States is a rich country with vast farmland producing an abundance of food for domestic use and for export all over the world. Although much of our food is shipped from huge corporate farms, family owned farms still provide the freshest food. Support your local farmers: "Buy Fresh, Buy Local."

35. American Space Exploration
NASA, The National Aeronautics and Space Administration, was established on July 29, 1958. It has led Americas efforts in space ever since. Its mission is to pioneer the future in space exploration and scientific discovery.

36. Statue of Liberty
The Statue of Liberty stands on Liberty Island in New York Harbor. It was a gift from the people of France and was dedicated on October 28, 1886. It has become an iconic symbol of freedom and of the United States of America.

Solutions

1. Map of the USA

2. The US Capitol

3. American Bald Eagle

4. Route 66

5. Sheriff's Badge

6. Country Square Dancing

7. Rodeo

8. Buffalo

9. Silver Dollar

10. Jack-o'-Lantern

11. Lighthouse

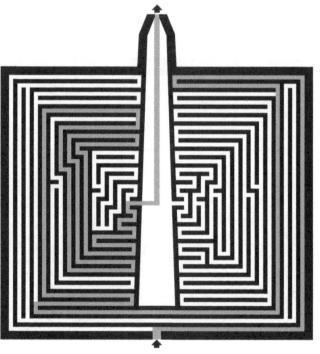

12. The Washington Monument

13. George Washington

14. Minuteman

15. Lewis & Clark

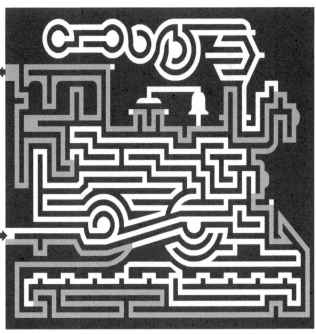

16. American Railroad

17. Jamestown

18. Baseball

19. Football

20. Martin Luther King Jr.

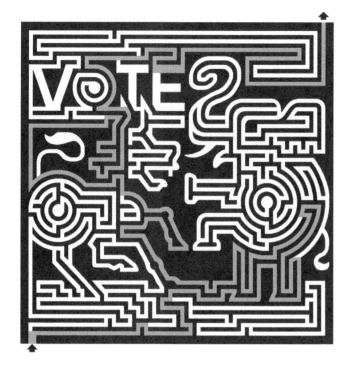

21. Right to Vote

22. Sitting Bull

23. The Stagecoach

24. First Flight

25. Amelia Earhart

26. Abraham Lincoln

27. The Civil War

28. American Soldier

29. Paul Revere

30. Elvis Presley

31. The Liberty Bell

32. American Indians

33. The Wild West

34. American Farming

35. American Space Exploration

36. Statue of Liberty